10/06

3.3
0. 5

Hammerhead Sharks

ABDO
Publishing Company

A Buddy Book
by
Julie Murray

VISIT US AT
www.abdopub.com

Published by Buddy Books, an imprint of ABDO Publishing Company, 4940 Viking Drive, Suite 622, Edina, Minnesota 55435. Copyright © 2005 by Abdo Consulting Group, Inc. International copyrights reserved in all countries. No part of this book may be reproduced in any form without written permission from the publisher.

Printed in the United States.

Edited by: Christy DeVillier
Contributing Editors: Matt Ray, Michael P. Goecke
Graphic Design: Maria Hosley
Image Research: Deborah Coldiron
Photographs: Digital Vision, Minden Pictures, NOAA (National Oceanic and Atmospheric Administration)

Library of Congress Cataloging-in-Publication Data

Murray, Julie, 1969-
  Hammerhead sharks / Julie Murray.
      p. cm. — (Animal kingdom)
  Summary: Briefly describes the appearance, habitat, behavior, senses, and life cycle of the three main kinds of hammerhead sharks.
  Includes bibliographical references (p.) and index.
  ISBN 1-59197-319-8
    1. Hammerhead sharks—Juvenile literature. [1. Hammerhead sharks. 2. Sharks.] I. Title.

QL638.95.S7M87 2003
597.3'4—dc22

                                                                    2003056031

Contents

Sharks

    Sharks have been around for more than 300 million years. These fish swam the seas back when dinosaurs walked the land. Today, there are more than 350 kinds of sharks.

    Some fish have bones. Other fish have **cartilage**. Cartilage is softer than bone. It is bendable and lightweight. Sharks have cartilage instead of bones. Other fish with cartilage are skates and rays.

There are many different kinds of sharks.

Hammerhead Sharks

Hammerheads are easy to spot among other sharks. Their oddly shaped heads are wide and flat. Scientists say this shape helps the shark turn fast and move easily in water.

Hammerhead sharks have a wide head.

There are nine kinds of hammerhead sharks. Most kinds are named after the shape of their heads. They are:

1. bonnethead
2. great hammerhead
3. scalloped bonnethead
4. scalloped hammerhead
5. scoophead shark
6. smalleye hammerhead
7. smooth hammerhead
8. whitefin hammerhead
9. winghead shark

What They Look Like

Hammerhead sharks can be many sizes. The great hammerhead is the largest hammerhead shark. It grows to 20 feet (six m) long. Adult great hammerheads may weigh as much as 500 pounds (227 kg).

The scalloped bonnethead is the smallest hammerhead shark. It grows to about five feet (two m) long.

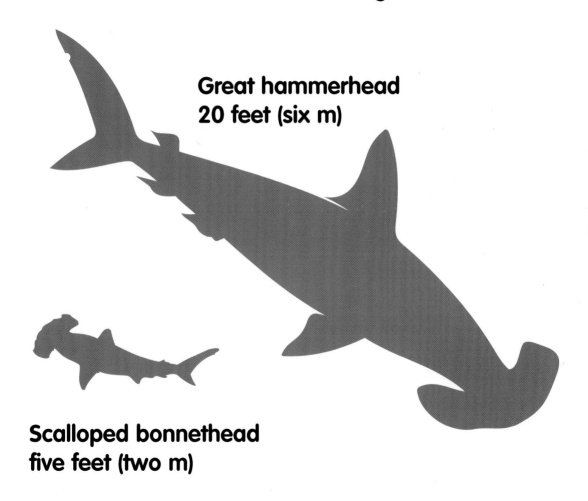

**Great hammerhead
20 feet (six m)**

**Scalloped bonnethead
five feet (two m)**

The hammerhead shark has an eye on each side of its head.

A hammerhead shark may be gray, olive-green, or brownish-gray. There is an eye and a **nostril** on each end of its head. The hammerhead's mouth is on the underside of its large head.

Hammerhead sharks have a strong tail and **fins** for swimming. A dorsal fin is on the shark's back. Two big fins on each side of the shark are its pectoral fins. Fins help sharks steer themselves.

Fins and a strong tail help hammerhead sharks swim.

Where They Live

Hammerhead sharks live in warm waters around the world. Some hammerhead sharks **migrate**. They travel to warmer waters when the seasons change. Other hammerheads stay in warm waters all year long.

Great hammerhead sharks live alone. Some other kinds of hammerheads live in large groups. These groups are called **schools**. Hundreds of sharks may live in one school.

A school of hammerhead sharks.

Hunting And Eating

Hammerhead sharks are **predators**. They hunt and eat other animals. Stingrays are the hammerhead's favorite **prey**. They also eat fish, lobster, squid, and crabs. Hammerheads eat other sharks, too.

Scientists believe the hammerhead's wide head helps it find food. Widely spaced eyes and **nostrils** may help it sense **prey**.

Sharks have keen senses for finding prey.

Shark Attacks

It is true that hungry sharks sometimes bite people. Sharks bite when they are scared, too. However, people are not natural **prey** for sharks. Shark attacks are not common. Less than 100 people suffer from shark bites each year.

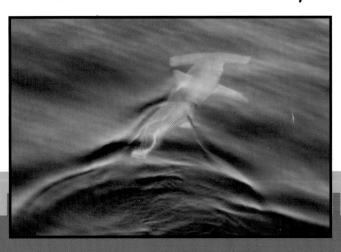

Deadly Teeth

Inside a shark's mouth are many rows of triangle-shaped teeth. Each tooth has tiny, sharp points along each side. The shark's sharp teeth can cut very well.

A hammerhead shark may lose thousands of teeth in its lifetime. When a shark's tooth falls out, another tooth takes its place.

A Sixth Sense

    Sharks have the same five senses as people. These senses are sight, smell, touch, taste, and hearing. Unlike people, sharks can also sense **electricity**.

    All animals have an electric field around them. So, hammerhead sharks can use this sixth sense to find **prey**. It helps them find animals hidden in sand or murky water.

Sharks can sense an animal's electric field.

Shark Pups

Baby hammerhead sharks begin life inside eggs. These eggs are inside the mother shark. After hatching, the baby sharks stay inside the mother and grow bigger.

Baby sharks are called pups. Female hammerheads have between five and 40 pups at one time. Newborn pups are between eight and 28 inches (20 and 71 cm) long. They have a soft head that hardens as they age.

Young hammerhead sharks learn to find their food.

The mother shark leaves her pups as soon as they are born. The shark pups must find food and take care of themselves. They grow into adults on their own.

Shark pups grow up to be deadly predators of the sea.

Important Words

cartilage matter that is tough and bendable. A person's ears and nose have cartilage.

electricity something that happens in nature. Lightning is one form of electricity.

fins flat body parts of fish used for swimming and steering.

migrate to move from one place to another.

nostril an opening of a nose.

predator an animal that hunts and eats other animals.

prey an animal that is food for another animal.

school a group of fish swimming together.

Web Sites

To learn more about hammerhead sharks, visit ABDO Publishing Company on the World Wide Web. Web sites about hammerhead sharks are featured on our Book Links page. These links are routinely monitored and updated to provide the most current information available.

www.abdopub.com

Index